know the game

Riding

produced in collaboration with the
BRITISH HORSE SOCIETY

ISBN 0 7158 0520 7

CONTENTS

Introduction	
Early Lessons in Manege or School	
The Simple Aids and their Application	10
Balance and Suppling Exercises	14
Work on the Lunge	15
The Trot	16
The Canter	20
Turn on the Forehand	23
The Simple Change of Leg	24
First Jumping Lessons	24
The Schooling Seat: The Cross Country Seat	29
Work in the Open—The Gallop	30
More Advanced Jumping	31
Adjusting the Stride	31
Competitive Riding	32
The British Horse Society	36

FOREWORD

This book has been written primarily to help those of you who are new to riding. I hope that by the time you have read the book thoroughly you will have realised that there is a lot to learn if you wish to ride well; but you should also realise that you will not get the maximum enjoyment out of riding until you do become a competent rider.

It is equally important that you should learn how to look after your horse or pony. A horse is not like a car which just needs petrol and oil and a periodic servicing; a horse is a living creature which can give you much pleasure and enjoyment but which in return needs to be cared for properly. If you own a horse or if you intend to buy one and you do not know how to look after it properly you must get help and advice.

The British Horse Society has been established to give you that help. As the national governing body for equitation and horsemastership, it is responsible for organising and administering the national training and examination scheme and for encouraging the care and welfare of horses and ponies. It is also responsible for looking after the interests of riders generally. The Society wants to help you—but it needs your active support. Only by receiving your support can we ensure a healthy future for riders, for horses and ponies and for riding generally.

> Nigel Grove-White
> Training and Development Officer
> *British Horse Society*

INTRODUCTION

Learning to ride is a discipline which becomes a pleasure, but like any other sport or game it must be taught on sound principles.

Good teaching must start by establishing mutual confidence. The beginner must have confidence in his instructor and in his horse, and in due time he will develop confidence in himself.

The instructor must engender this confidence in the first instance by his own appearance, voice and manner. He should be capable of imparting his knowledge clearly in short simple sentences, and by giving practical demonstrations.

In his training of both horse and rider he applies the same general principles. All training must be methodical and progressive, always improving, but never going beyond the capacity of the pupil.

Confidence in the horse can only be established by starting the beginner on a quiet well-mannered animal that will stand still when being mounted, and is obedient to the simple aids at walk, trot and canter.

To place a novice rider on a green horse is utter folly, and inevitably leads to unhappy results in both horse and rider.

To gain further confidence the first few lessons should be in an enclosed arena, either riding school or manege, and the pace must be a walk.

To encourage beginners to relax all muscles, quiet rides outside should be organised, if this is possible, riders riding in pairs, at a walk under the supervision of the instructor.

The Balanced Seat

The rider's *seat* in the saddle is his position when mounted. The horse has a natural centre of gravity which alters a little according to what he's doing, and the pace at which he is travelling. This centre of gravity is just behind the withers, and our first task is to place the rider in the saddle so that his balance is aligned as near as possible with that of the horse.

Then we must develop his natural balance, suppleness, and muscular ability so that he can stay *in balance* with the horse whatever he is doing.

The rider must learn to conform to the horse's movements, and to do this he must be relaxed and supple. The seat must be firm without any excessive action of arms, legs or body, therefore the suppleness must be a controlled suppleness. The seat must be completely independent of the reins. A rider without this firm and independent seat cannot convey clearly his requirements to his horse; confusion follows, and if any result at all is obtained it is a mediocre one.

The development of the seat takes time.

The Saddle

To help the rider sit in the right place a modern central position saddle is a *must*. The front arch or pommel should be high enough to clear the withers, the rear arch or cantle should be slightly higher than the pommel. The deepest part of the saddle should be well forward, the waist narrow and the stirrup bars recessed.

Good saddles are expensive, so it pays to go to a firm which has a reputation to consider.

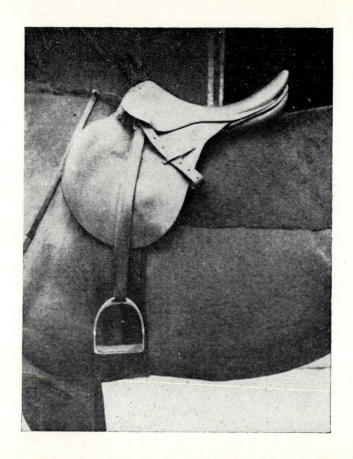

The Rider's Position at Halt and Walk

The first few lessons in placing the rider in the correct position are of the greatest importance. Bad habits contracted in the early stages develop the wrong muscles and are therefore extremely difficult to put right.

We have said that the centre of the horse's equilibrium is just behind the withers; it is also the strongest part of the horse's back for carrying purposes, the further back you go the weaker it becomes; the loins must be entirely free of any weight. So, the seat bones must be in the deepest part of the saddle with the crotch well forward. whilst the fleshy part of the buttocks is pushed to the rear; I emphasise that the rider must feel his seat bones in contact with the saddle. This can only be achieved if the back is straight and the shoulders above the hips. The thigh, knee and lower leg hang naturally down close to the saddle and the horse's sides, without clutching or gripping. The length of stirrup should be adjusted by the instructor so that there is an angle to the thigh when the foot is placed in the iron. This angle depends on the shape and length of the individual rider's legs. The short thick thigh will require a shorter leather than the long thin one. This is where the experience of the instructor is vital; a stirrup that is too long will cause the rider to tip forward and feel insecure; a leather that is too short will cramp the knees and hips and encourage the rider to push his seat to the rear.

Careful adjustment is necessary, and if the knee is kept relaxed the lower leg should come naturally back and stay softly by the horse's side, just behind the girth, the *inside* of the rider's boot against the horse's sides.

The stirrup iron should be on the ball of the foot, the toe slightly out at a natural angle, the heel slightly lower than the toe to tension the calf muscles. The ankle acts as a buffer to help cushion the seat in the saddle when moving at the various paces. Therefore the ball of the foot must rest on the tread of the stirrup iron and not push against it, the ankle joint and knee must at all times be supple: whether you are on the ground or on a horse balance starts at the balls of the feet; so to be *in balance* the heels, hips and shoulders must be in a straight line with the stirrup leather vertical.

The rider's head must be held high with the eyes looking forward, this helps his natural balance, and should give the feel of stretching up with the body. By *riding tall* you ride lightly thereby conforming to the horse's movements and not impeding them.

Grip

Any attempt to pinch with the knees must be avoided at all costs. The knee and thigh must lie softly against the saddle, with the lower leg naturally back. This may cause the knee to come away from the saddle in the early stages, but it does not matter. As the rider's muscles develop over a period of training the seat will deepen in the saddle and the knee, thigh and lower leg will adhere closely to the horse. One rides mainly by balance and suppleness but grip is often necessary. It is a momentary thing and should become a natural reflex action when required. Grip starts with the inside of the calf below the widest part of the horse's barrel. Gripping in this manner gives the rider a feeling of great security without stiffening the knee or hip joint.

Hands

Educated hands can only be acquired over a period of time when the rider has developed a firm and independent seat; but from the beginning the rider must be encouraged to have quiet hands which always have respect for the horse's mouth. The first essential is to ensure the reins are held correctly. With a single rein it should pass between the little and third finger, through the palm of the hand and over the index finger where it is firmly held by the thumb. The thumb is on top with the knuckles naturally to the front.

The upper arm should hang without constraint and the elbow should form a gentle curve from the top of the shoulder down to the fingers. The rein should be of such a length that when it is taut the elbows are just in front of the hips, and the instructor should see a straight line from the elbow—little finger—along the rein—to the bit.

One of the first essentials of good hands is that the elbows should be soft.

Having placed the rider in position and taken up the reins the horse should be walked round, so that the rider can feel the movement of the walk. At the ordinary walk the horse swings his head; a light contact must be maintained by keeping the elbows soft and following this movement. The rider's hips will swing with the horse's hips, thus getting the feel of the movement, and encouraging the body to conform and be supple. Provided the horse is going in the required direction and at the desired pace, the hands must always follow the movement. In this way hands begin their education.

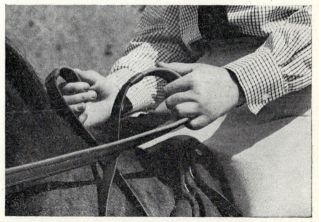

EARLY LESSONS IN MANEGE OR SCHOOL

A manege or indoor school should be well-proportioned, and if used mainly for schooling should be based on the measurements of the international dressage arena. For teaching, 40 metres by 20 metres is ideal. The manege must be correctly marked so that riders learn to ride accurately. See diagram.

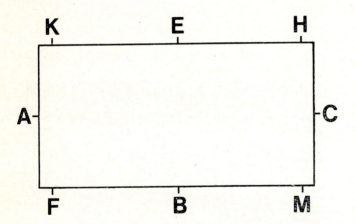

Mounting and Dismounting

The horse must learn to stand still when being mounted. The rider must check his saddlery and length of stirrup before mounting.

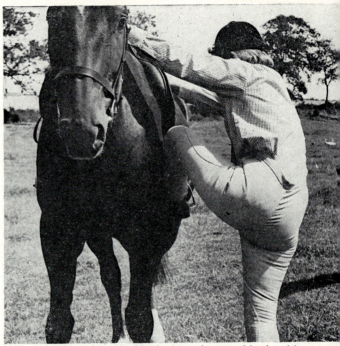

To mount Stand level with the horse's near side shoulder, facing the rear; with the left hand take up the reins until they are just taut, then grasp the horse's mane or wither. With the right hand hold the stirrup iron and place the left foot well into the iron with the toe pointing down. Grasp the back of the saddle with the right hand.

Then spring up from the right foot, straighten the left knee and swing your right leg over the saddle, at the same time transferring your right hand from the rear to the front arch of the saddle. Lower yourself gently into the saddle. Finally take your right stirrup, and a rein in each hand. Your horse should continue to stand still until he is given a definite indication to move forward.

Dismounting Take both feet out of the stirrup irons. Place both hands on the front arch of the saddle still retaining the reins, lean the body forward and vault off on the nearside of your horse, making sure that your right leg is well clear of his back. Land lightly on your toes, facing forwards.

THE SIMPLE AIDS AND THEIR APPLICATION

The trained horse learns to obey certain signals which we call *aids*. The horse must be taught to obey them only when they are applied correctly. Therefore, it is essential that riders study and practise the application of these aids. Only by using the aids clearly, distinctly, and in harmony will a good performance be obtained. The natural aids are: the voice, the hands, legs and weight of the body (through the seat). The artificial aids are whips, spurs, martingales, etc.

The Voice The horse's hearing is very sensitive and the use of voice, particularly during training, has a very definite effect on the horse. A soothing voice will calm, whereas a loud bullying tone will frighten and upset.

Weight The weight of the body can be very effective, both on increasing and decreasing pace and on changes of direction. The difficulty with many riders is that, lacking a truly firm and independent seat, the weight is used inadvertently, and impedes the free movement of the horse instead of helping it. The novice rider should be trained to keep his weight central and even, on both seat bones, and allow his weight to follow the natural movements. The more advanced rider will eventually be capable of influencing these movements by a judicious use of his weight.

The Legs One often hears horsemen talk about *good hands*, but rarely about *good legs*. The legs have two important functions in riding well and in training. First, acting with a pushing effect close to the girth they create and maintain impulsion, without which your horse is like a car without petrol; and secondly they control the hindquarters. By using one leg with greater strength just behind the girth the hindquarters of the trained horse can be moved laterally.

But first, the horse must learn to accept the rider's leg—sensibly: in the same way as he learns to accept the bit, by a continuous even contact. The lower leg therefore, must be held close to the horse's side with just sufficient steadying by the knee and ankle joint to keep the inside of the rider's boot in contact with the horse. Any movement of the lower leg must mean something, so unless an aid or signal is being given the lower leg remains still and in contact. When the novice rider begins to gain control of his lower legs he should carry a schooling whip or switch, about three feet long, so that the light action of the leg aid can be re-inforced by a touch of the schooling whip. A common fault is to draw the lower leg too far back when using it. This only serves to irritate the horse causing him to switch his tail, and often produces a loss of impulsion.

The legs should always be used close to the girth place with a light squeezing action, the rider's heel remaining depressed, to tension the muscles of the calf. When the leg is drawn back it should only be a matter of two inches.

Hands It has already been stated that the first essential in educating the hands is a firm and independent seat. The next is finesse in their use. As in using the legs the hands should ask for an action always in exactly the same manner to avoid confusion in the horse's mind.

To develop the normal *feel* of the horse's mouth and the movement of the head and neck the rider must first have the correct length of rein, and then learn to follow the movement maintaining a soft continuous contact the whole time, the reins being just *stretched*.

Good hands are normally passive, and always quiet. They yield to increase pace and resist to decrease pace. The hands should never pull; they only resist sufficiently to overcome the horse's resistance, and cease the moment the resistance ceases. Both hands should never be used with the same strength: for example, on a decrease of pace one hand maintains contact and the other asks with slight give and take action of the fingers. Educated hands will produce an educated mouth. Riders with heavy insensitive hands never feel the pleasure of the perfect mouth, when the bit is held softly and the horse obeys the slightest indication of the rider.

Harmony of the Aids

The first and most important function of the aids is to produce and maintain controlled forward movement. This forward movement is guided and developed by the rider's hands through the medium of the reins. The horse therefore must be driven forward towards the bit at all times, and not the bit pulled back by the rider's hands towards the horse.

The first lesson then to be learnt in applying the aids is that the seat and legs precede the hands, whether on an increase or decrease of pace. This ensures that the horse will engage his hocks before making a movement.

Diagonal Aid In changing direction the same principle applies. The rider must first understand that the horse must always look in the direction he is going, and in simple turns and circles his hind feet follow in the track of the fore feet. For example, the aid for turning to the left. First the legs insist on forward movement, then the inside hand, the left, in this case, asks the horse to just look to the left, the outside hand must work in harmony and allow the bend without losing contact; the outside hand will also control the pace on the turn; the outside leg, the right, drawn just behind the girth controls the quarters; the inside leg, on the girth helps the bend; both legs maintain forward movement. This is called the diagonal aid, where each hand and each leg have a different task but work in harmony to produce a smooth change of direction. This aid is used throughout equitation, and the emphasis with which each leg and each hand is applied can produce many different effects, but in the early stages of training the rider must be taught to apply the aids so that they do not work in opposition to each other. If the right rein asks for bend the left must yield to allow it; if the right leg acts to move the quarters, the left first yields to allow the movement and then resists to regulate it.

Study and practice are essential, and only by riding a reasonably well trained horse will the novice rider learn to feel the effects of his aids.

Application of the Aids

The rider must first learn to carry out simple school exercises at the walk. The walk is a calm easy pace, and the novice will have no difficulty in maintaining the correct position which is the same as the position at the halt, except that the rider's hips swing slightly to the rhythm of the pace, and the hand follows the movement of the head and neck. The weight is even on both seat bones, the shoulders slightly in front of the hips, the head is held high with the eyes looking forward. Looking down rounds the shoulders and slackens the loins, making the seat sloppy and unstable. By looking forward at your own height the back and loins will be erect and effective.

Moreover, this work must be done accurately, so learn to ride to the school markers and think ahead.

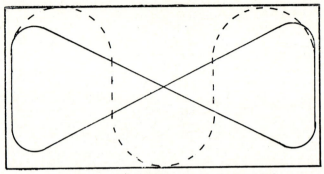

Long Figure of Eight, Serpentine to the Long Sides

Large circles

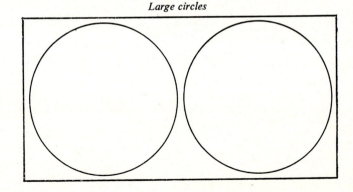

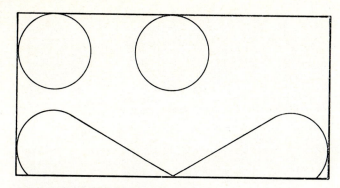

Small circles, half circle from the corner

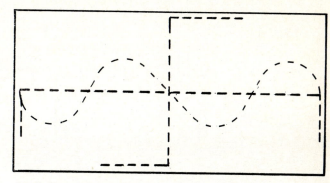

Simple Turn and change down the centre line serpentine

Keep the weight on the seat bones so that the legs and hands are free to be used lightly and independently.

First the aids for increase to walk and back to halt must be practised; then the aids for a simple change of direction. The diagrams give examples of school movements to be practised.

All exercises must be carried out at the walk until the rider is sitting with confidence and applying the simple aids, and achieving these simple movements with reasonable accuracy.

This work should be varied by the novice rider being taken for quiet walks out of doors in company with at least one other quiet horse. This gives confidence, helps relaxation and develops a sense of rhythm and balance.

BALANCE AND SUPPLING EXERCISES

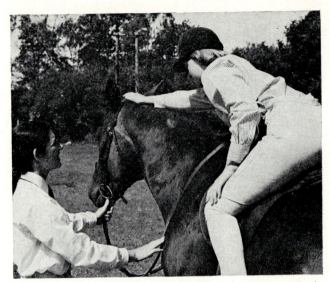

At this stage simple physical exercises can be carried out by the rider to help supple up any part of the body that may be stiff, and at the same time these exercises will improve the natural balance and increase the strength of the seat.

These exercises can be tiring on unaccustomed muscles, so firstly they should be carried out by the instructor with good humour, which encourages relaxation, and secondly, they must be done regularly but for very short periods.

All exercises should be practised at the halt to begin with.

To Supple the Neck Muscles Rotate the head in a clockwise direction six times, then anti-clockwise.

Keep the shoulders and hands still.

To Supple the Ankles Feet out of the stirrups, and rotate the feet six times both ways. Again keep the rest of the legs and the hands still.

To Supple the Shoulders Reins in the left hand: rotate the right arm in a vertical circle; keep the left hand still: change hands.

To Supple the Waist Drop the reins on the horse's neck. Place the left hand on the horse's mane and the right hand in rear of the saddle towards the horse's croup. Now by turning the upper body change hands fairly quickly, with the eyes looking to the front and then to the rear. Keep the lower leg still.

Suppling the Loins Drop the reins. Let the arms hang down by the sides. Now bend down and touch each toe alternately to either side, returning each time to the upright position. Do not place the disengaged hand on the horse's neck: keep the lower leg still.

There are many other exercises that can be devised by the good instructor for individual faults and stiffnesses, and if they are carried out conscientiously have beneficial results.

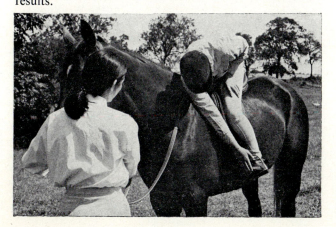

WORK ON THE LUNGE

At an early stage in training the novice rider, working the rider on the lunge for ten minutes every day helps to develop the following essentials:
(1) Improves the balance
(2) Strengthens and deepens the seat
(3) Promotes independence of the hands and legs
(4) Develops a sense of feel and anticipation

Lunging the rider can be dangerous and do more harm than good, unless the following safeguards are observed.

The Instructor has sufficient experience and technique to lunge a horse well and at the same time observe and correct the rider's position. He must be capable of judging the experience and ability of his pupil, and adjust the duration and variety of the exercises to the rider's physical fitness.

In the beginning all work should be carried out at the halt or walk with stirrups. The balance exercises mentioned in the previous chapter can all be used when working on the lunge.

The Horse The main object of working a rider on the lunge is that the rider has no need to be apprehensive about the control of his horse; it is controlled by the instructor.

Therefore the instructor must ensure that the lunge horse is quiet on the lunge under all circumstances. He must stand still when required and move on the circle at an easy walk and trot.

The safety of the rider must be the instructor's first concern, so with the quiet horse must go the correct equipment.

Equipment   An enclosed circular space, or in an enclosed school.
   (1) Well fitting lunging caveson
   (2) Plain snaffle with reins
   (3) Adjustable side reins
   (4) Lunging rein at least 22 feet long. Fitted to central 'o' of caveson.
   (5) A lunging whip
   (6) Brushing boots to protect fetlocks
   (7) A good central position saddle

Work without stirrups should begin as soon as the rider is confident and fit enough to work without muscle strain. Lunge lessons should be of short duration, and each lesson must be systematic and progressive if it is going to be of permanent benefit.

THE TROT

The best way to learn the feel of the trot is *on the lunge*. The rider should hold the pommel of the saddle with two fingers of both hands. Then he must sit upright as for the position at the halt, but as the horse is going forward a little more, the shoulders should be just slightly in advance of the hips: the hips and knees should be relaxed, and the feel the rider should get is one of being thrust deeper into the saddle at each trot stride. If the pupil is allowed to lean back the thighs, knees and heels will work upwards and the whole position will be out of balance and behind the movement.

The horse must be trained to go at a slow steady trot with a well-defined rhythm.

This slow sitting trot must be practised with and without stirrups.

The next step is to ride *free* at this pace, and now the pupil must learn to maintain a light contact with the mouth during this sitting trot. Holding the saddle with one hand can be a great help.

The Rising Trot

Sitting down at a slow trot gives the novice rider the *feel* of this two time rhythm, but it can be very tiring to the beginner. School movements, therefore, should be practised in Rising Trot with the horse going forward more energetically in what is known as the Working Trot. The act of rising is achieved by inclining the body slightly forward from the hips and allowing the body to leave the saddle on one beat and coming back in the saddle on the next beat. Practise this motion standing still and the rider will discover how much he must bend from the waist to rise without effort. It will also be felt how much the lower leg governs the upper part of the body; it must be kept behind the perpendicular and close to the curve of the horse's body, if rising is going to be achieved without hauling the body up by the reins. To ride lightly and be in perfect balance the stirrup leather must be vertical, the weight of the body must travel down sufficiently to allow the heel to remain just below the toe, the back must be flat, and the eyes looking forward, with the hips and shoulders going upwards and forwards in the same plane.

The Diagonals

We have said the trot has a two time beat: this means the feet come to the ground in pairs; the off fore and near hind being the right diagonal, and the near fore and off hind being the left diagonal.

In the rising trot the seat comes down into the saddle on one diagonal and leaves it on the other. If the rider stays continually on one diagonal the horse's muscles are not evenly developed, and he will become stiff and awkward on one side. Therefore the rider must learn to change the diagonal frequently, by making an extra *bump* in the saddle, then glance down at the horse's shoulder when the seat comes into the saddle and one can soon tell which diagonal one is riding on. In the school or manege it is the custom to change the diagonal when changing the rein.

The Hands at the Trot

At whatever pace the horse is going the hands belong to the horse's mouth.

In rising trot the body goes up and down but the horse's head remains still, therefore the hands must remain still, and not go up and down with the body. This calls for softness in the elbows, which will allow the rider to maintain a steady even contact on the horse's mouth.

Work at the Trot

All exercises performed at the walk must now be introduced at the rising trot, starting first with the increase and decrease of pace from walk to trot and back again. In preparing to trot the reins must be shortened slightly, then both the legs applied lightly close to the girth and the hand eased. The horse should advance straight forward actively into trot; if the response to the rider's leg is not immediate then the schooling whip should be applied sharply to reinforce the leg aid. It is a fundamental of all schooling that the horse goes actively forward from the leg. When the correct pace is achieved then commence rising. The lower leg must stay close to the horse's side, passively, but ready to sustain the pace.

To reduce pace the rider prepares his horse by sitting and closing the legs slightly; this ensures that the horse uses his hindquarters; then decrease to a walk by resisting with one hand a little stronger than the other. The walk must be achieved with a steady head carriage, the body straight and no resistance. The hands will then take up the rhythm of the walk. Turns, circles and inclines must be practised so that they are executed smoothly and accurately, with the horse's body bent on the line of movement, and with the same speed and rhythm.

This work, done under the watchful eye of a good instructor will teach the rider how to apply the aids in harmony; by the *feel* of his horse he will learn how much leg to apply when increasing and decreasing, which side of the horse needs a stronger leg aid when turning; how much resistance is necessary on one side or the other of the mouth. Only by *feel* and by tactful application will the rider learn to refine the aids and get the best from his horse.

The rider must concentrate on five things.
(1) His position, which always requires constant attention, until the right muscles are developed
(2) That the horse goes actively forward from the leg
(3) On a decrease of pace the hindquarters must be engaged and the head carriage steady
(4) The horse's body is bent on the line of movement
(5) The pace is active but the rhythm is even.

Periods of concentrated school work should be short, otherwise the horse will become resentful or bored, according to his temperament.

Therefore, periods of work in the school should be interspersed with quiet hacking and easy work over undulating ground. This gives a pleasant break to both horse and rider, helps them to relax, and improves the natural balance and anticipation of the horse's movements. Work in the open must be kept at a walk to begin with. Eventually however, all work done in the school must be practised outside.

Sitting Trot

The rider has learnt the feel of the slow sitting trot on the lunge, but has continued to work in rising trot until the suppleness and firmness of the seat improves.

The sitting trot must eventually be practised at the true working trot pace; in fact, with a well-trained horse and rider, there should be no change in the speed or rhythm of the trot in rising or sitting. This must not be practised too soon or for too long periods. The rider's back must remain straight, and the action of the trot must be taken up by suppleness in the waist, knees and ankles. The rider must avoid pinching with the knees, as this only stiffens the whole body and defeats the object of sinking deeper into the saddle.

It is always good practice to hold the front arch of the saddle with one hand for a few strides if the rider feels unsteady or feels his seat slipping to the rear.

On a horse that is supple and swings his back the trained rider is much more united with his horse at sitting trot; the *feel* is greater, and the aids can be applied with greater influence and precision.

In sitting trot the elasticity of the pace can be developed. Having practised successfully the working trot sitting, a certain lengthening and shortening of the stride should be attempted, and gradually improved upon. At first the rider will find the horse will attempt to quicken the stride and increase the speed; this is the natural reaction, but this the rider must avoid. As the horse goes forward from the legs to increase speed he should meet a gently resisting hand which will check the speed, but the impulsion created will encourage the horse to lengthen a few strides: when this is felt, the leg action should cease and the hands resist a little more, bringing the horse back to his working trot. This lengthening and shortening the stride by the rider, requires great tact in the harmony of the aids, and provided one asks for just a little at a time the scope and brilliance of the trot will gradually improve. And, of course, the rider, our main concern at the moment, will develop a greater feel for his horse, improve his seat, and apply the aids with greater sympathy and co-ordination.

Trotting Poles

When the rider is capable of working in a reasonable rising trot then I am a great believer in the use of trotting poles to improve the seat. From the rider's point of view, trotting poles produce a more robust action; this teaches the rider to look to his balance, makes him realise very quickly when he is out of balance, and will teach him by feel when to tighten or relax his muscles. Also, in fairly slow motion, it will give him the feel of the horse's head and neck action when he is going over a small fence.

From the horse's standpoint, it teaches him not to get excited or suspicious at the sight of coloured poles: this then is a good education for his jumping. It also teaches him to balance himself in his efforts to avoid treading on a pole.

These are valuable lessons for both horse and rider.

As in all new lessons we introduce it in the easiest and simplest way, starting with one pole on the ground. The poles must be heavy, and not easily moved; this teaches the horse to respect them. Place the pole in the track on one long side, about the B or E marker. Now the rider should walk his horse over the pole. The rider's body should bend slightly forward from the waist, his head up and eyes looking beyond the fence. The legs remain still, but close to the horse's sides; the hands maintain a light elastic contact throughout. Generally, the horse will stretch his head and neck down and forward; the hands must follow this movement without any restriction, except a continuous contact. Now place a second pole about five feet from the first and practise the same exercise.

The next step is to trot over the poles, with the rider in rising trot. This position will carry the rider's body naturally forward, and the rider will stay in balance, and at the same time feel the accentuated *swing* of the horse's back. Six poles should eventually be used.

If the rider's position becomes unsteady, the stirrups may be shortened one or two holes for this exercise. Constant attention must be paid to the rider's position. Firstly, this is an exercise where the rider must learn to keep his legs still. Establish the trot well before the approach to the poles, then keep the legs still when negotiating them. The rider must look forward and keep the back flat. Angle and knee joints must be supple; the hands must maintain a light but constant contact.

This lesson has great value in itself, but is also a necessary preliminary to jumping. Practised properly, it will be found that jumping comes much more naturally to both horse and rider. When the rider can negotiate the poles in rising trot with a good position, then simple exercises may be practised to strengthen the seat and improve its independence of the hands. These exercises may include:

(1) Sitting Trot, with and without stirrups. The shoulders must remain in front of the vertical, and the rider must sit *softly*, so that his weight does not interfere with the *swing* of the horse's back.
(2) Without reins. Hands in riding position
(3) Folded arms
(4) Hands on hips

These exercises will also give the rider greater confidence.

THE CANTER

Before the novice rider is allowed to attempt the canter, his seat should be reasonably firm at sitting trot.

The canter is a faster pace with a complete change of rhythm, this rhythm being a swinging three action. To maintain his seat the rider must synchronise with this motion: also, in the canter we find the horse swings his head, whereas at the trot the head was still. Because of the change in rhythm and the increased speed the novice will tend to *hang on* to the reins more tightly, thereby interfering with this natural swing: the result usually is a stronger pulling horse, and great apprehension from the rider, causing a general stiffening of his body, which is exactly the opposite of what is required.

The instructor's aim therefore must be to canter the pupil on a quiet school horse, the rider first holding the front of the saddle with one hand, and the reins in the other. The firmness and security thus produced will enable the rider to apply the aid to canter, and also help him to adapt to the new motion. The canter should be attempted first from a corner; this makes it easier for the rider and positions the horse for a correct canter. To canter then, on approaching the corner, from a sitting trot, both legs are applied, with the outside leg behind the girth, a contact being maintained on the horse's mouth. Keep the body upright as the horse strikes off. The hand holding the reins follows the head, the other hand pulls the seat firmly into the deepest part of the saddle.

Position at the Canter

The position of the lower leg remains the same, just behind the perpendicular, with the inside of the boot against the horse's sides, the toe on the stirrup iron and pointing forward at a natural angle and the heel just below the toe. Both ankle and knee accept a greater weight and act as shock absorbers. The back must be straight and the head held high so that the hips are supple and can take up the swinging action of this new pace. As the pace is a little faster, the rider's shoulders are in front of the hips, and the weight on the seat bones is light. Suppleness can only be achieved by keeping the back straight. The body of the truly supple rider appears not to move when cantering, but with the stiff rider there will be an excessive swing.

The hands must follow the movement of the head with a soft elbow, as they did at the walk.

When the rider can conform to the movement of the canter then the correct aids can be taught and school exercises carried out.

Aids to Canter

To understand the aids to canter the rider must have a knowledge of the sequence of footfalls at this pace. The canter is a pace of three time, and a horse canters with a left or right *lead*. For example: right lead sequence is as follows:

(1) Near Hind
(2) Left Diagonal Together
(3) Leading Foreleg—Off Fore
(4) Moment of suspension, when all four legs are off the ground.

With a left lead the sequence is the opposite of course.

To enable the horse to turn smoothly, quickly and safely, he should always canter with the inside foreleg leading. This can be easily observed; the inside foreleg and inside hind leg are in advance of the outside pair of laterals. Cantering to either lead the pace must be a united one. If it becomes disunited, caused by loss of balance, or insufficient schooling, it will be seen that the diagonal pair has been broken, and the inside foreleg and hind leg are not in advance of the outside pair.

The aids applied must produce this right or left lead as desired.

In a well-schooled horse the aim when striking off into canter should be to keep the horse as straight as possible, as in all other paces. However, it is easier for the young rider, or the young horse, to learn these aids if one applies them at a corner or on the circle: this *positions* the horse correctly and encourages him to strike off on the desired leg.

From sitting trot to begin with, the aid applied is as follows:

> Inside hand asks for a slight bend towards the leading leg; outside hand controls the bend and pace;
> inside leg, strongly at the girth, prepares the canter;
> outside leg just behind the girth signals the canter with a soft 'nudge'. Careless use of the outside leg, such as swinging it back and kicking, will cause the horse to swing his quarters in, and may cause confusion later in his training. On the well-trained horse the use of the outside leg is minimal.

Transition from Canter to Trot

In this decrease of pace it is important that the rider uses a strong seat and leg aid, combined with an asking hand to obtain a balanced trot immediately, and not a shuffle forward for two or three strides. The head carriage must be steady and the horse's body straight. Progressive school movements should be carried out on both leads.

TURN ON THE FOREHAND

As the rider's ability in applying the aids improves so he must practise movements which call for great tact in the application of the hands, and strength in the use of the seat and legs. Such an exercise is the turn on the forehand. A normal turn or change of direction asks the horse to look in the direction he is going, with his hind feet following in the track of his forefeet.

In training the rider the turn on the forehand is done from the halt, as follows: turning across the school in the normal way the horse should be halted at right angles two yards from the track. The halt must be balanced with the horse standing squarely on all four legs. In a turn to the left the horse must just look to the left, so this hand asks for a little bend; the outside hand checks forward movement and controls the outside shoulder; the inside leg

drawn slightly back pushes the quarters to the right, the inside hind leg moving laterally in front of the outside hindleg; the outside leg controls the movement of the quarters. When a quarter turn has been completed the horse should be asked immediately to walk forward.

If carried out correctly the horse pivots his quarters round the inside foreleg, which should move up and down on the same spot. This is a fairly simple exercise which encourages the use of each hand and each leg in a separate action and increases the rider's control over the hindquarters.

THE SIMPLE CHANGE OF LEG

Before this exercise can be attempted, the rider should be capable of striking off into canter on a straight line. This is best done on the incline across the school K-M or H-F or vice versa on the other rein.

The true simple change must be done through the walk. A canter to walk transition is a very high standard of schooling, so in the early stages this can be done progressively through the trot, but there must be one or two paces at the walk before striking off on the other leg.

In this exercise it will show whether the rider has practised correct canter aids, by observing if the quarters remain straight. The simple change should also be practised from a twenty-metre circle, and on straight lines.

FIRST JUMPING LESSONS

Riding over fences should be included in the education of any horseman. Not only does it improve the rider's position and sense of feel, if the preliminary stages are carried out correctly it gives pleasure to the beginner and creates enthusiasm. Provided the rider has learned to sit correctly and in balance over trotting poles it is a small step to introduce a low rail or cavaletti about 18 inches high which will cause the horse to jump.

Naturally, the rider must learn to sit over a jump without loss of balance or hanging on to the reins, and this can best be done if we study the action of the horse over fences.

On the approach the horse lowers his head slightly and stretches his neck. This allows him to balance himself. On take-off the horse shortens his neck, brings his hocks under him, and makes his spring upward and forward. As he *tops* the fence his body is rounded with the head and neck stretching out to their fullest extent: as he lands the neck is shortened and the hindquarters come underneath for the first stride of the *getaway*. It must be obvious that once the horse has taken off the rider must not interfere with this natural leap either with his body or his hands.

To stay in balance the rider should shorten his stirrups by two holes, thus closing the angle between hip, knee and ankle joints. In jumping and riding across country there is more weight on the ball of the foot and less on the seat bones; this enables the rider to sit lightly and stay in balance. The knees and ankle joints act as buffers to absorb the body movement.

As the horse takes off the rider bends slightly forward from the hips, keeping his head up and eyes looking forward, with his back flat. The seat bones stay close to the saddle, and the rider should avoid any tendency to straighten the knee and stand up. Over a small jump the forward movement of the body is negligible; over a bigger jump it is greater, but should never be exaggerated. Experience and practice will teach the degree of movement required.

Hands The objective should be to maintain a light contact throughout, and to achieve this the rider's hands must conform to the movements of the horse's head. On take-off the horse shortens his neck slightly—the rider's hands come back; as he tops the fence he stretches his head and neck down and out—and the hands follow; on landing the hands return to their original position.

The First Jump

Now we can practise our first jump. Four trotting poles about five feet apart should first be trotted over a few times to get the rider sitting in a balanced position ready to jump. Now place a cavaletti 18 in. high about 9 ft. from the last pole and trot in as before. The horse will make a small jump, and the rider will have no difficulty in following the movement. When this can be negotiated with confidence a second cavaletti can be placed 18 feet

away to give one canter stride and another jump. Any number of cavaletti can be used at varying distances: two close together will form a spread, but cavaletti should not be placed on top of each other as this can be dangerous.

Only by adhering explicitly to these exercises, and practising them in a progressive manner, will the rider learn to sit well over fences and develop his eye for bigger obstacles which will come later.

A variety of small practice jumps up to 2 ft. 9 in. high should be available for the next stage. Solid fences that are fixed are essential. The horse learns to respect them and therefore there is less danger of accidents. Poles, brush fences, tree trunks, banks, ditches, etc., fences which are upright and others which involve a spread.

The rider should plan a series of small fences to jump in sequence, involving simple changes of direction. Until control is improved it is advisable to trot between fences, and particular care must be taken to apply the correct aids for changing direction, and for increase and decrease of pace. In other words do not neglect the work on the flat. The horse must continue to be a pleasant ride so good schooling on the flat is even more essential. It is important that the rider is mounted on a well-balanced free-going horse throughout these early stages of jumping.

THE SCHOOLING SEAT: THE CROSS COUNTRY SEAT

When training the rider at the basic paces of walk, trot and canter, the student is encouraged to ride with a longish stirrup leather compatible with security and steadiness, so that he may develop the correct muscles which will give him a deep seat, and also enable him to use his legs to their fullest. As the paces are comparatively slow the body is upright and in balance; most of the rider's body weight is on his seat bones and very little on his stirrup irons. A secure, well balanced seat is the eventual result. From this firm position the aids can be applied lightly, independently and accurately. When riding over fences or across country at the gallop, the seat must stay firm and in balance and this is best achieved by shortening the stirrups two or three holes. This not only closes the angle of the thigh—body and lower leg, but greater weight is taken on the stirrup iron and less on the seat bones throughout the phases of the jump, but the seat bones should always be ready to come down onto the saddle, if the rider requires to drive a *sticky* horse into his fence.

The position at the gallop will be explained in the next section.

WORK IN THE OPEN—THE GALLOP

The gallop is a pace of four time, and is obtained by increasing the canter until the diagonal is broken, thus causing each foot to come to the ground one after the other. There is a moment at the end of each stride when all four feet are off the ground; this is called the moment of suspension. As in the canter the horse must lead with the inside foreleg.

At this pace, on a free-going horse the rider's seat should leave the saddle with the body inclined further forward, allowing complete freedom to the horse's back and loins. The rider's weight is taken on the lower part of the thigh, down to the knee and the ball of the foot. The lower leg stays just behind the perpendicular and close to the horse's side. The knee and ankle joints act as shock absorbers, enabling the rider to conform to the pace with lightness and comfort for both.

The shorter stirrup causes the buttocks to go a little to the rear, enabling the rider to maintain balance, whilst the position of the knee and lower leg gives security, the stirrup leather remaining vertical. If properly in balance the rider should not have to maintain his position by hanging on to the horse's mouth.

When riding a *sticky* horse or on the approach to a fence, the seat comes down into the saddle, although the shoulders remain forward and the back flat. In this position it is easier to feel what the horse is going to do. to anticipate, and if necessary overcome any resistance. Also, the legs can be used more firmly, to send a horse into his fence if it is necessary.

Riding in the open must be practised at all stages of the rider's training. In fact, all exercises practised in the school must be performed outside.

But first, the rider must walk, to enable him to gain confidence and produce relaxation. Walking over rough ground, gentle slopes, etc. is good training for both horse and rider, teaching the horse to balance himself, and the rider conforming to this movement. Hills and slopes of varying steepness, small streams, and ditches cause the horse to be careful where he puts his feet; it makes him extend and collect, improving his natural balance, so that when faster paces are begun and obstacles begin to be ridden over, greater confidence will be felt, and the rider will learn to ride with boldness and determination into his fences. In riding outside, the rider must endeavour to follow the principles he has learned in the riding school.

The horse should always be between hand and leg, whatever the pace, and not allowed to go into a fast trot or sloppy canter.

Ride straight whenever possible, but look ahead and always avoid bad going.

MORE ADVANCED JUMPING

In our early jumping lessons the instructor should concentrate on first getting the rider to conform to the horse's movement, then on improving the position. Bad habits that go uncorrected in the early stages will get worse as fences get bigger. The rider's role should be a fairly passive one, with legs and body still with no excessive movement. Changes of direction should be soft and easy so that the horse can still be ridden forward without loss of impulsion.

Fences may be raised gradually as confidence increases but at this stage should not reach a height or width that calls for any real effort from the horse.

With regular jumping of a series of small fences the rider will begin to see his stride and develop an eye for distance, but the rider's task at this stage is to bring his horse to the point of take-off, in balance, at the right speed, and with sufficient impulsion to clear the fence. He must learn to use his hands and legs in harmony in order to gain or maintain this necessary impulsion and balance.

ADJUSTING THE STRIDE

Seeing his stride means the rider can judge some distance away, whether the horse is going to arrive in the take-off zone on a full stride, and if not, remedy the situation by lengthening or shortening. Any adjustment must be done smoothly, and as far away from the fence as possible. A great deal can be learned by practising with a distance rail. Place a small fence or cavaletti three true strides away from the fence. Practice over this a few times then remove the cavaletti. The rider should attempt to arrive on the line where the cavaletti stood, and make no adjustments after this line. With practice judging the distance can be developed. Very few riders can always *arrive* correctly at every fence, therefore, most riding over fences, except for a few experts, must be a partnership based on the sound training of horse and rider.

COMPETITIVE RIDING

Showing

For the learner rider and for the young horse a short season of showing is very valuable experience. Many good horses and riders, both in the showjumping and eventing worlds, start off by showing in the working hunter classes.

A show horse needs a lot of preparing before he is ready to enter the ring, but if his basic schooling has been sound, then he will walk, trot, canter and gallop when asked to do so. In working hunter classes he will be expected to jump a number of small fences. If the horse will do all these nicely and come back in hand still maintaining a light contact with the bit, he will win more prizes than better looking horses that are not so well trained.

If the rider's basic training has been well and thoroughly carried out, and the horse has received a thorough grounding in his schooling, then the simple movements required in the show ring can be performed with ease, and with the lightest indications from the rider.

The rider must now study his horse. It must be physically fit so that, however hard the ground, his legs will be strong enough not to trouble him.

If he is of an excitable nature it is as well to get to the show ground early when the horse should be ridden about very calmly and quietly perhaps for one or two hours. Quietly walk, trot and canter in and out of other horses and as close to the main ring as possible. Steady work on the lunge is often a better way of quieting an animal; work on the circle has a very soporific effect on most horses. This is called riding in, and is a necessary preparation before entering the ring. It depends so much on the horse's temperament how much riding in is necessary, but it is always a sound principle to arrive at the Show Ground early. A plain saddle is the best for showing, with the flaps not too forward cut, so that your shoulder can be clearly seen by the judges. An ordinary Weymouth double bridle should be used. Boots, bandages, martingales are not allowed. When once in the ring the rider must obey the orders of the ring steward. He must ride with due consideration for others but should try to get into a good position so that, when he passes in front of the judges, there is no other horse blocking his view.

Horses will then be called in and formed up in line for the judges to ride. During the time of waiting make certain your horse is standing well. After he has been ridden by the judges the saddle can be removed and he can be rubbed over with a rubber.

Take the reins over his head and lead him up in front of the judges: again, see that he stands well. He should then be led away at a good walk for about twenty yards, turned about to the right to keep his hocks under him and trotted sharply back.

When the judges have finished their inspection the saddle can be replaced and the horse re-mounted. If the rider is lucky enough to win a rosette you smile and thank the judge. If not, you still smile and put it down to **experience**.

Show Jumping

Show jumping is now very professional, and unfortunately many young people take to this branch of the equestrian world without a proper grounding in basic teaching with the result that if any success is achieved it is short-lived.

If horse and rider have been trained on the lines laid down earlier in this book they should be capable of entering their local riding clubs' show jumping competitions, and then newcomer competitions. This is good experience for both, and if the horse has a big jump and is bold, then show jumping could be his game. But as in showing, the rider must make careful preparations.

Read the rules of your particular competition; they should be known by heart. See that your horse is well ridden in before you enter the ring. Walk the course and study each fence, and the track you are going to ride. Measure the distance between combination fences and know what your own horse's stride is. Keep your horse calm, and ride your first show jumping competition so that it is a pleasant experience for both horse and rider.

Event Riding

Undoubtedly among the most popular equestrian activities today are the One-Day, Two-Day and Three-Day Events. Horse Trials combine the three basic skills of training the young horse: dressage, show jumping and cross country work.

The average well-made horse who has been trained on sound lines should be capable of taking part in a novice one day event, but here again competitive preparation for both horse and rider is essential. Riding Club Dressage Tests and small show jumping competitions test the state of training and show how well the combination of horse and rider go together when they appear in public.

Three Day Events

There is a very large gap between one and three day events. Whereas the one day event is within the reach of most well-trained horses, the three day contest calls for an exceptional horse with boldness and stamina, plus speed, and with the right temperament to accept this type of training. Furthermore, a great deal of time is required to work up to this standard, and this is usually beyond the capacity of the average person. If the keen rider and horseowner will take the time and trouble to train themselves and their horses on sound lines up to a standard where they can both enjoy whatever activities they go in for, they can consider themselves to be accomplished horsemen and horsemasters.

THE
BRITISH HORSE SOCIETY

Do YOU know what the British Horse Society is?
Or what it does?

Did YOU know that our responsibilities include:

The Pony Club for young riders
The Riding Club movement for adults
Advice on careers with horses
Publication of instructional books and pamphlets
The improvement of tuition standards throughout the country
Combined Training; including One, Two and Three day events
The promotion and control of Dressage
The co-ordination of Horse and Pony Breed Societies
Advice to the Government and Local Authorities on equestrian matters

All this is in YOUR interest, but it costs money. Why don't you help promote riding by joining the B.H.S. now?

The British Horse Society,
The National Equestrian Centre,
Nr. Kenilworth, Warwickshire CV8 2LR.

J. Ward, Dewsbury, England